Billy Takes A Break

Margie Harding

MOTHER ASKED BILLY TO FEED AND WATER THEIR DOG, JEB.

BILLY GAVE JEB FOOD AND THEN TOOK A BREAK TO READ A COMIC BOOK.

MOTHER ASKED BILLY TO MAKE HIS BED.

BILLY PULLED THE COVERS UP AND THEN TOOK A BREAK TO PLAY WITH HIS TRAIN SET.

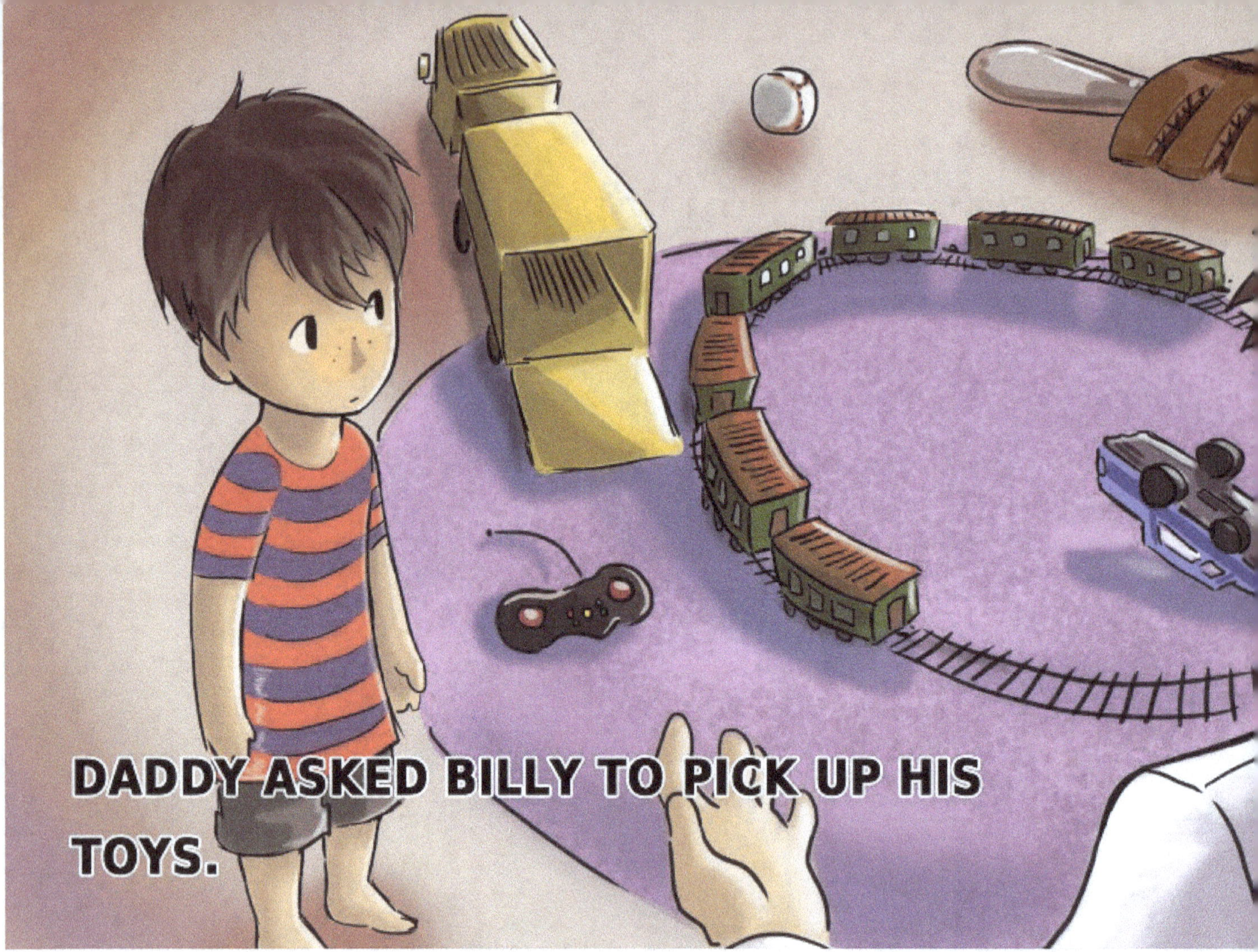

DADDY ASKED BILLY TO PICK UP HIS TOYS.

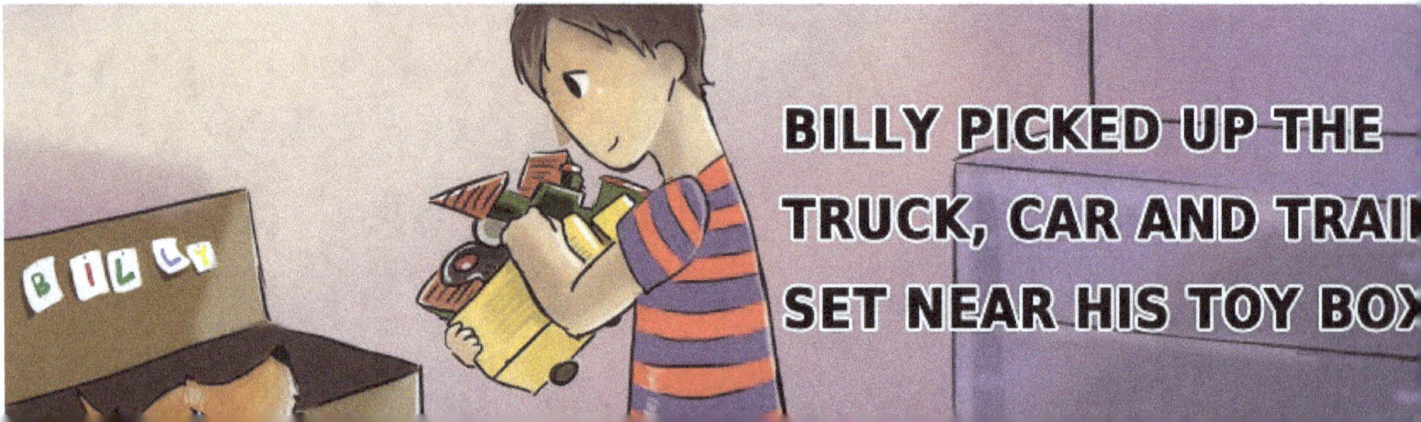

BILLY PICKED UP THE TRUCK, CAR AND TRAIN SET NEAR HIS TOY BOX.

BILLY WANTED A SNACK OF MILK AND DONUTS.

MOTHER GAVE BILLY MILK.

BILLY WANTED TO RIDE HIS NEW BIKE.

DADDY PUT AIR IN ONE TIRE AND THEN TOOK A BREAK TO WATCH A SPORTS SPECIAL ON TELEVISION.

DADDY DIDN'T ADJUST THE SEAT OR PUT AIR IN THE OTHER TIRE. BILLY COULDN'T RIDE HIS NEW BIKE.

BILLY WANTED MOTHER TO MAKE COOKIES.

MOTHER TOOK OUT THE SUGAR, FLOUR, SHORTENING AND VANILLA.

MOTHER TOOK A BREAK TO WRITE A LETTER.

MOTHER DIDN'T TAKE OUT THE MILK OR EGGS, MIX THE INGREDIENTS OR BAKE THE COOKIES.

BILLY HURRIED TO GIVE JEB A DRINK.

www.ingramcontent.com/pod-product-compliance
Lightning Source LLC
Chambersburg PA
CBHW081400080526
44588CB00016B/2561